Square Blue Bucket Full of Trouble

Poems by

Rich Ives

Cyberwit.net
HIG 45 Kaushambi Kunj, Kalindipuram
Allahabad - 211011 (U.P.) India
http://www.cyberwit.net
Tel: +(91) 9415091004
E-mail: info@cyberwit.net

Printed at Repro India Limited.

Acknowledgments

Arsenic Lobster: One Eye Opened

Crack the Spine: Seagulls Marching Before the Tide

Self-Portrait, in Absentia

Danse Macabre: Domicile

Del Sol: Oklahoma Love Song

But What Do You Really Think?

Another Love Poem

Eclectica: Scavenger

Kill Author: Since I Can't Paint Landscapes

Some Good Advice

Monongahela Review: Dick Tracy Cap Pistol, South Dakota, 1959

Pirene's Fountain: Plank

Posit: Several Islands Have Appeared

Shaking Hands with Children

Red Fez: Contemplation of a Small Speckled Egg Frozen into a Whiskey Glass

Requited: Several Islands Have Appeared and Swimming Is Possible

"Seagulls Marching Before the Tide" was also included in the Crack the Spine 2013 Anthology.

Contents

I. Departures Small Enough to Arrest You

One Word for All the Trouble

The crowd does not whisper but sighs.
In the eyes of the undone, the next is last

and is taken deeply aside, as if recognized,
one leg and one leg and one leg and mouth open,

broken in the cast of its thrown intention.
I have been discovered by a word.

Could I be myself and only I become
departed, as each wheel must finally arrive,

the terms of engagement never structural,
syntax flopped about like a squeeze-toy?

If the mind moves in and makes of it something other,
we shall have to translate what the mind sees,

pieces of it broken off the shore defined by clouds,
still sleeping in sips of November,

one door closed in a language under the curve
that seeks the tongue, the stairs tuning

a gathering of bald spots, doomed to be perfectly happy
in a world entertained by exquisite suffering.

The one word *lost* is not lost, but the word for
found is never crowded, never in such excess,

just as the word *begin* can only sip from
what we do next to save the singular crowd.

Civilization

There in the back yard claiming the stone I sit on to rest and
think, nose up and attentive, stands an unlikely coyote. I've never
seen one here, though once at 2 AM I heard the howl so raw

it must have been a kill, a winner,
something dead for dinner.

A breeze-caught tuft of hair on his shoulder erupts like an
explosion. As he returns to the earth we share, he's limping, his
right front paw favored like a sleeping child. He feels me watch-
ing, slowly raises his eyes and locks on the window that allows me

to know this reasonable doubt
waiting patiently to be let out.

If I think of him standing there on the edge of my gentleman's
life, my thoughts enter the trees and imagine what's waiting while
I stay right where I am. Perhaps I long for a home between the
unknown and the known, in the shared space he has entered,

turning it to the other side,
knowing better than I when to hide.

He's poised but not afraid, as I am, of something less obvious to
watch, darker than a wild thing, as it discovers what I am and
what I am not, watching the wild thing watch. I separate my
surprised thoughts from this as I lope

away from the domestic space
I have ghosted with no human grace.

Bartender, County Kerry, 1888

daft bugger was after having the best of it she was
her alcohol stomach a loose sack slung low out of fit
but a right good shine this sot with her lamp and cause
wasn't but a pint would take the harm out of it

her alcohol stomach a loose sack slung low out of fit
like the coldest unnecessary day sent us beyond grace
wasn't but a pint would take the harm out of it
beyond the fields behind stones still galloping in place

'twas the coldest unnecessary day sent us beyond grace
and give us a good snacker in the gob she'd blunder
beyond the fields behind stones still galloping in place
some kind of a misplaced warmth moving under

and give us a good snacker in the gob she'd blunder
wantin' to know if she's dead where's the paradise
some kind of a misplaced warmth moving under
daft bugger was after having the best of it she was

Portrait of a Marriage, Alaskan Coast

1.

it was not my painting
thinking it could not remain

and I said I didn't know
when I coached it to confess

who had spoken
it was too beautiful

it almost saved me
and that wasn't enough

and I couldn't leave it alone
where something was not

I said no and didn't save
what I wanted a terrible success

so I asked it what is art
helpless before the question

it wouldn't respond until later
thinking it was me

I couldn't leave
because I could not go back

from what I knew I wasn't
so I couldn't go there

couldn't dive into myself
as strange as what happened

a self from myself
its beauty burning

2.

it's true she'd been working
he'd been living up to her promise

yet falling the day she came home

to feel sorry for

leaning out its nothing else
it knew when waking

hard at divorce
the balance of the dark not

alone knowing enough
and not
the bottom of the day

one part of many together
it looked like something held

beneath the surface   when there was
no surface yet told them   so much to feel

the next man was kind   by telling her no
his raw smell gentle   persistent nerve and

acceptance assuring her of   the subsequent experience
spilling the moment approaching   with only partial focus

3.
it's true he'd been hard working   forced to hands lifting
                                       promises
from one cold day to another   gone dumb with repetition of

the art of numb money flung   canvassed oil from earth
pigments brushed onto a marriage   the way they touched

each to each moment laid down   in a mind they created
from a platform on the surface   of a labor's need

a respectable attempting to hold   more than dollars with
survival grit plucked from   cable and beam absent

the dream that brought them   the farthering day
impending departure   its own warming need

of anticipation while   critical of the next best
another awaited
light down low   in the light's throat

4.
it was not my painting   so it asked me what is art
thinking I could remain   helpless before the question

its gallery of others waiting
future soaked and

pulled fully oiled here
slick with another day's journey

steep nights longer
farther from yourself

with loaded brush to open slowly
to the wild lights

to illuminate blind
intimate with absence

for lovers with more than one
dedicated to irony

from the ocean
back to more and on to

the dark that draws you
where the other waits

full of yourself
northern enough

to pass by so
much longer in answer

Pussycat, Your Whiskers Are Dirty

Marriage bestows on love the tenderness of a departing guest.
—Sean O'Faolain

husband number one is wearing a silver lining he's pouring
a moonlit corridor don't get me wrong I just want you
to have the right misunderstanding

don't attach yourself to the hidden husband
his containment provides no inner journey and self-reliant security
turns a fence post to a slowly drawn sword

husband number two could be cactus and voles
could be paper lanterns could be sleeves
could be testing at the bomb site and
he could be too sure of himself at midnight
he could be the color of sleep and listening

right now you think you have a choice
but you have to take them all one at a time like fish on a line

husband number three comes with a mother
who places a lovely disposition between you and his pants
trousers she calls them blustery and puffed as if
something rich and amusing might fall out
and it does when she's busy
entertaining the gardener

the state took back husband number four
seems he was husband number two more than once
and no longer eligible for a bed without bars

it comes from the lamb and it comes from the hilltop
and there is no scholar to read its wool or perch upon its rounded head

maybe telephone lines maybe mixed drinks and maybe wool hats

you didn't know you were a verb until after
from the viewpoint of the noun you've become

that's how uncertainty knows when to eat

the last husband looked around to see what he was made of
for he was not the center of himself
and there you were
a little too perfect to not become
and since you were looking for someone just like him
he went looking too

My Uncle Was Killed in the War

though I didn't know what I was doing there   I grew up in
South Dakota farm attics dreamed of   the silhouettes
waterfowl I could shoot down and planes   I couldn't kill
while fathers were cast to the opposite   and could

but didn't come down
soon enough came girls' offerings one breast   and another
before I knew how to take offerings and
the one I   saw the most
was the loveliest because I saw its movement   towards not
                                                   exactly
inside me but something I was inside   how I want this
and I thought   to ask me

and not come down

a death-in-the-mud generosity let me have this   quietly as we
died and died and fought over the beliefs of   lost others in
                                                   our failings
each to enter each and quite fully enough   and without
                                                   preference
if there was play in it we didn't know   we were still
                                                   doing this

and didn't come down

outside the barn door still applauding   the wind's
                                                   breathless

entrances and replacements while one hungry   war fed us
                                                 departure
left the camps leaking and aging with the young glad to be rid of
parents who had paid returned and paid since   the nothing that
                                                 was final

but didn't come down

every day the young bodies stuffed into sacks   to let us out of
                                                 this
didn't belong to me or even my father's   brother who
                                                 gave me to my
first camera before leaving for   history which
                                                 shut
my long shuttered eye and he jumped   and I left him
                                                 there

but didn't come down

Dick Tracy Cap Pistol, South Dakota, 1959

Where I grew up, conversation would seem to be
the only relief from landscape. You could follow
phone lines, sagging just enough to seem human,
except they were everywhere, and we were not.
You'd figure some important things got carried
across, field to field, but mostly they didn't.

Aunt Elizabeth was glad to hear from you, for example,
and the Junior High bake sale a week ago Tuesday
was a modest success, and Sunday the children slept
right through the sermon on the earth's great bounty
and Reverend Smith farted loudly and never even
missed a beat and then spoke even more seriously
in case anybody was left listening, but outside,

we were the ones listening, and we told each other again
what we already knew, and we secretly marveled over
the gossipy meadowlarks, the ring-necked pheasants
living three wives to a family right there in our midst,
and the Hutterites living self-sufficiently like communists
in the very next county. Our own busy-ness became
everybody's and almost kept us from following ourselves

into the indifferent landscape. We thought it would, but
for such a long time it seemed a week in Disneyland
and a fishing trip to Canada were enough away to keep us
from getting lost in the party-line hum hung up along
the gravel roads, but you had to memorize everything
out of place, everything small enough to arrest you.

Ode to Snow

I wish I didn't know about the inside of things
that keep me occupied with their beauty.

Behind the field behind the barn behind the farmhouse,
a cow nearly barks and goes on eating and eating again.
There's mint on his first breath, and he breathes again,
and the milky wildflowers in his stomachs take over
the job of making plants feed plants.

It's dark and no one's there. Is that you?

The end of everything I know is there, and snow,
early, floating down the too-warm air
as it touches and departs.

I wish I didn't have to think, but I want to know
that I've decided not to think about it
instead of just falling in and scrambling back.

It's dark now, and no one's there, and I might be
only what I'm still thinking, but the wind is behind me,
and there's a way to get inside, where
it's surprisingly warm and easy to melt

and go on without thinking.

Domicile

I don't understand the marker I see
between my house and my neighbors,
but I know it changes me.

The sun is there, and the horizon,
and the late shadows of the tree boughs
across the empty alley seem to run

towards me like a slow river, and suddenly
it seems as if my grass is too neat
and my body is leaning, slovenly,

towards the end of something more
than this anchored space, rent
by deed and fence from the earth.

Or should I borrow understanding from
the encroaching city, measure my place
in row upon row of boxed families come

loose from themselves, planted here
where progress means restraint, taste
and grooming, where a healthy fear

must find a courtroom and hold back
anything it might achieve by abandon,
the word that falls from my lips' slack

grasp of vision, leaning with my rake
unmetered toward the word for leaves,
which alters its paper pounding of the stake?

Something held speaks to me in this last light,
offering permanent space between a canyon
of absence, a marker on the distant height,

and this certainty I return to with tools
to shape its lost arms to pretty green sleeves
pinned to the clever confidence of fools.

Such certainty is a silent beauty I've known
only once before in a cemetery gone wild
at the edge of anything I've been after.

On the Occasion of Your Temporary Departure

I wish I had your air of nonchalance.
It would come in handy when I hide from
my interrogators, whose methods of torture
don't include Frango mints or long warm baths,

and if your lovely arrogance were a little less prickly,
I'd want to rub it up against my submissive enticements
and set them on a shelf in the neutral cooler to see
what kind of terrifying awards might develop,

and I might even welcome your glorious anger if
it could be counted on to erupt at the sight of
Salvation Army bell-ringers and couples holding
more than damp hands while eating pink donuts,

but I don't think I want your generosity,
a quality of giving I don't really understand,
like insouciance or Chlamydia or a millionaire
who leaves it all to a barky Pomeranian,

and I don't think I want your wedding shoes, which
have forgotten themselves in the closet again, much
like your wedding guests and your memory of your
blossoming husband trimming dangerous hydrangeas.

If I consider what I'll miss, it would be your deep
recognition of surface textures and your collection
of certainties displayed so wordlessly. If only I
could be so thoroughly myself while still breathing,

but since you're coming back, I'll just miss some things
one might wish to have self-destruct before the beauty
of your absence, things like your measured warmth
or your calculated compliments or the beauty of

your presence, which shall reward me soon enough
since that which one wishes for seldom arrives, even
when it's another departure, and the odds are against
accidental suicide or atmospheric kidnapping or mercy

terrorism or someone else who loves you enough to appreciate
all these subtle qualities of character, someone whose welcome
back wouldn't back up before it wears off and already knows what
I've just learned about how annoying I can be when you're not here.

II. Abbreviated Misunderstandings of Exaggerated Perceptions

My Space

the room I lived in was inside
the room I previously
 inhabited

and the space I was in
might have still been the
same space

someone else had been in
long before
I didn't fancy myself unique
but just a bit
wordy and therefore inside
myself also

I didn't always have enough
to do with the room in the
room

for a relationship which
I've accused myself of
on other occasions
the space I was in
might not have been spacey
enough to hold
like all of the sarcasm
my partners contributed

and so I tried to get outside
to the space in the room
which was not the only space
where there was room to
admit

I could alter
the room's outer to its inner
and

adjust the different way
I would have to inhabit
for new territory and
its old-fashioned hospitality

the problem appeared to be
of course sometimes
its door could be
leaving but actually open
for filling the room
with leaving outside and
then

leaving the room open to
weather and
uncontrollable urges and
interpretation

that was why   it was not actually
the whole room   the space of any moment
could be exchanged in   if only one could trade
one's perspective for   another circumstantial
some chosen other   alternative moment

which doesn't explain   what I'm doing here
maneuvering the space   I have left for myself
in the alternate room   which does not contain you
when you have inhabited   so long my dear spaciest
territories and given me too much   space I mean

just because you moved out   which doesn't mean
I've moved you out of   the room inside the room
the space you've taken with you   has become
more abstractly   necessarily more distant
than it was when you spaced out   inside my space

I have only to forget   what I'm doing here
to discover new territory   inside the room
if I decide to do something   to your space
then it's still in my space   even as I move it
out of the already accomplished and   is space inside my space

I'm just wondering now   if I have to live here
if opening a new house   in the room
holds my place in my space and   then I'll find my space but
might not replace the room   environmentally
altering the context within   which I continue replacing
                                      with space

Mistaken Identity

Venezuela, 1972

I wasn't there. It wasn't me
who claimed to have seen winged phantoms
dancing on the cooling air. I had no
glass eye, no memories trapped in amber.

The cornclowns tasseled with silk,
their dried-up shirts clattering,
yellowed teeth too large for their heads,
weren't any part of my experience,

though I can understand, like you, how
that might have affected someone else.
You can't make me name the blue
that hung over the evening like a sky

but couldn't long be seen because
the government troops frightened it.
No one, to my knowledge, heard the piccolo
enter separately from the nightbirds.

The helmets of copper-headed conquistadors
were not arranged artfully across the dining
room walls and there were no stone-groined
statues guarding the vestibule. Not even

the gorgeous black Steinway is available
to my memory now because I was not there.

Still, there is something I came back with
from my absence, though I certainly don't

wish to dwell upon its beauty, although
it still haunts me as if it were, in fact,
all I had ever known of the evening after
an impulse to become someone else.

Nearly an Ethnic Joke, Then, Is It?

A gun and a suicide enter a bar together holding a rabbit by the ears. The rabbit says, *I ear you shot off your mouth again* and the gun says, *I've been open since closing time,* and the suicide tees off into a lake of soft blue bullets where words have been laughing endlessly at their limitations.

The gun brings light to the endless words, goes silent, empties the rabbit, says, *There ain't no more bleedin' pie now is there, Love* and cuts open the suicide with surprising incisors and lays out the organs on the bar with toothpicks to mark the decay. Poor bastard was almost dead anyway.

Real humour is brought to cover the mistakes. A sudden laboratory opens the bullets like a harsh clothing exchange falling from the story of the bar, which just lies there bleeding like a donation and lines the punches up for laughter and a chaser of sarcasm no one finds offensive enough,

and the square blue bucket of insult enters the serious bathroom window with a can of what next, a can of not this, a can of not anything like this, and a can of people wanting freedom for believers, and a can of everything else, and a can of disgusting laughter inside another can of you're welcome.

But What Do You Really Think?

Someplace between other days, I found my
self but not who I was. I put the corners of the box
in the middle. Sometimes the wrong man is always right.

She needed another bag of sleep, a local darkness,
the flutesong of just a little water and no more.
She needed a little folderol, a little who-ha in her bucket.

She looked hard, so I tried to look hard
at something else that wasn't so hard.
Of course there's a paradise, but

it's not ours. Was she really the kind of woman
you don't want to go home to after
you fucked someone else?

I didn't tell the truth because
I didn't know it, and that's what saved me.

By that time she had said so many
nice things about me that I
wanted to be him so I could
appreciate myself.

It's true I was uncomfortable with who I was,
like an apparatus for removing the water
from the water.

Sometimes you need to hurt yourself
to take in what you already know. It's a good thing
the way I sleep is older than I am.

And I was watching myself doing exactly
what I was doing, which didn't make it
any more real.

Perhaps I'll call home and listen to myself
offer to listen to what I have to say
at some later date when I'm more available.

Listen. You can't do it alone, I said to
the whispering black poplars fencing the undertaker's yard.
Ask the summering oak tree outside his warm dark study,
I said to the finches in the ash trees.

He was an old guy up in his head
with all that had never happened to him.
His nurse's trousers are frequently frightened and damp.
Perhaps it was not the same interference as that other interference.

Another Love Poem

Ain't nothin' he says

the waddle of pasty white   fat man in the island sand
bruised clouds   spitting back among the
                                                     endless
mutinies of tamarinth seeds   recurrent sweetbriar pricks

holding beauty dangerous

a bowl of eggs with a single apple on top
a glass half filled with amber liquid

teaching a lesson   he'd never learned
it came on long and slow   left the same way
camouflaged to look like itself   paint splotches wearing fatigues

you can feed them what sleeps

on the anniversary of rolling pins   the date that did not go well
Susan spoke to herself   I've lost my personal freshness
said her fork was like   nothing to frighten the horses
                                                       but

too cruel to eat with

a pale green beyond any absent blue
at least a someone is driving the maybe truck

he needs her
he's hard like that

like a dog papa

but he don't even remember

to show him how he works
got a stone on him humped up
on her
her fingers were kinder

Old Woman Up a Tree

I used to think of you easily, Earth old friend,
but you have taken too many like retiring trees I also
love and listen to, but they have only one thing, and
it's beautiful but not as unexpected as what I heard from

friends gone home.

You're overzealous, and soon a last moment will greet me,
which I may appreciate, but that day has not arrived, and today
my friends haven't arrived either, and all I can do is listen to
the trees and perhaps climb one to see how it is to escape you

at least for a while,

the way I did before I thought about your intentions,
and I set leaves in my hair to get my naturalness noticed,
but not, I must admit, Taker of Friends, by you, and now
there is only one thing left to say. This belief I've stolen,

it's more than you intended.

And now as the sky descends and you reach up to meet it, I find
myself between my daily heaven and reality, unable to choose,
holding to the limb of a greater patience and waiting for sleep
to carry me away from my shrinking reach, and plant me

in the gravity of letting go.

Oklahoma Love Song

It's not that I asked for this or anything,
except what I have, to keep happening.
It's her plumply erotic youth, peachy with
unknowing ferment, just now beginning
to sweeten, to soften the curves.

O cowboy yodel, O Oklahoma sunset,
O O of astonishment and arms around,
I want to sing like the cork escaping.
I want to drink the wine buoyant and
bouncing across the room like bubbles.

I don't want to just try but be,
all my older openings opened,
my experienced fat roses coaxing
loose their thorns from my legs
and smoothing out the presentation,

a body's old clothes coaxing new
offerings like children uncertain.
It's not the ghost of the body
that haunts us but the ghost of
the thought that made the body.

On the Way to A Bar Joke

why do you need   your paving
green and never filled
this rest with no destination   containing a time
when thirst leaves

its sad and hungry   yesterday and
you know what
innocence already failed   by what will try
other villages desire

arrivals beyond dust   to see just who's there
when what happens
must be you   listening to you and
keeps talking

in the shadows of you   the broken roads
turning against
and there's nowhere to go   pebbles breaking
parental stones

needing to attach and march past   their sun it's enough
and could be mistaken
and sleep quietly in   your nervous laughter
so carefully forgotten

Nose/Hand/Foot

we try to lead children through life by the

as if teaching one part of the body
makes the others follow and we lift the

higher when our part is best
and when we find out things
best left hidden we're putting our

where it doesn't belong so if you can't
stay behind it then keep your mouth shut
and breathe deeply and wet the air with
your finger how perfectly it fits apply
a board to the bottom of the leg it's a shoe
apply the board to the

something blooms and grows heated
whether you broke it or not
but sometimes it's too obvious
and not about only what's in front of you
like the father with the wrong child's

in his fist a new game
of a frightened monster the

is like that you have to keep the

out of the way you have to sense when the

is about to lead you to release something
you didn't know you were holding inside
and wouldn't want to release any more
if you knew it might leave you older

and name itself with an accusation
that attached itself to your name
and became part of you at the farther end
and offered itself to nothing more than that word

III. Suspicious Offerings of Advice

[One Eye Opened]

there is little I know for sure

amazing endurance and sensitivity

can be swallowed and travel inside

but cannot know

  the one who hid it

is incapable of harboring resentment

can provoke nostalgia in its enemies

for those who would not exercise

some desire to defeat change

in a field in South Dakota

the great drought of 1959

had gathered so much heat

to meet my eye as I walked

a marble is indeed a
creature
can remain objective
reliably
can be betrayed
with a slingshot
can trip up the
heartless burglar

and memory's
childhood and
misconstrue this as
pleasure
through miserliness
or arrogance
wary of unexpected
arrivals

a marble in the
dying wheat
it could fall no
farther and rose
a dried-up pond to

the far end
dreaming the frogs and fish
and turtles and
younger boys

had managed to burrow deep

in the cracked lake bottom
to stay in my
thoughts
hiding away everything
offering the way life
does
I wrapped that marble in
a tissue to keep it's
light from biting
the crisp dried fallen tunic
a fallen stalk of
clattering corn

and I eyed the shriveling earth

but soon the pond was full and the earth
it was so full it was
leaking and
so much was floating that once
I decided it felt
good to eat
I sank down before death asked
into an ocean of
sloth
not moving anything
beyond even my
desirous thoughts

waiting for the world to digest

forgetting what I was for
I floated away
satiated on
a dream as it found me
oceans of dying
wheat
thinking about my relatives
gathered outside in

the dark
watching the heat lightning   we had to guard
closely

  shovels nosed into the all-too-available dirt

and I broke open a fist of potato   and lifted out the
satisfying skeleton
the dead river inside the white skin   that had grown
beneath its appearance
and put its promise away   in my stomach's
pocket now
another round earthly vision bruising a hardening romantic view

  in one of hunger's wrong directions

If It Wasn't for the Courage of the Fearless Crew

If you tell someone they're only acting that way, it's an insult.
If you tell someone they can't act, it's an insult.
If you tell someone they're not themselves, it's a warning.
If you tell someone they're full of themselves, it's a warning.

If someone really is only acting, they only mean it temporarily.
If someone really can't act, you'll know when they're not lying.
If everyone really isn't themselves, you won't even recognize them.
If everyone is really full of themselves, there's no room for you.

You have to know who you are to become someone else.
You have to know someone else to know who you are.
You have to try to be different to know what's the same.
You have to try to be the same to know what's wrong.

If someone else knows who you are, something's missing.
If you know who someone else is, they're not missing you.
If you know how to be someone else, you're not acting.
If you know how to be yourself, you've forgotten something.

The Right Thing to Say

One side of her absent, still on the street
where the car attached her to the pavement,
the cat turns, as if she could leave, in order to
get closer to the words I release, which she does
not understand, but wishes to follow, and

now I have to wonder where she's going
as a result of what I so deliberately
say. It no longer comes naturally.
I have to think when I speak.

I have no wisdom to help her get from
there to anywhere, no other life except
words, which lead me to her other side,
the one words seem to touch, even
when they can't be given back.

Perhaps One of Our Kind Will Find Us

Each night the flood dreamt our house
filled with its love. How far
from home our eyes drift, closed,
our secrets, opened. Let me ask you
because water doesn't answer:
Whose dream remains by morning?

And they all looked
carefully at the body.
Nobody knew who he was,
and they all looked because
perhaps they know who he is.

And death, having chosen
this man to translate
the note struck by a leaf
falling on moss, didn't know
what the water remembered.

Your imperfections more
than your beauty could challenge.

Blue trees were not available
though blue trees were everywhere.

Plank

The letters begin before I begin, repeating themselves,
connecting the one word to its possible other.
     —spray-painted on construction sight wall

1.
as in "to bridge between"—

equality disguised as direction
access as accomplishment

2.
as in "to pluck away at" (plank, plank)—

the crow or the banjo for example
thought of as instruments designed for elegies
and mournful cries of oppression with which
catastrophic errors are sometimes conceived

most expressive when indulged immediately
preceding a funeral

3.
as in "to walk the plank"—

one death placed in front of the other
held together by minimal gravity
deepening acceptance followed by
discovery of the fluidity of experience

see: graduation

4.
as in "a siding of"—

rough and fresh over soft and folding
clapboard sleeping in the covered wall
a skin thick with anticipated weather

a vertical personal sky stained with
an expectation of extended time
the someday gray of always waiting

5.
as in "to cover over"—

an expression of irony conveying certainty
often confused with the "frontier" version
("to place under the sidewalk" or
"to close the lid upon") which presumes
a clarity of conclusion seldom evidenced by the facts

see: metapoetics—risk factors
see also: suicide—projection and metaphorical abuses

6.
as in "slab"—

a substantial occupation of space
to be placed fat and chunked its volume
slapped flat weighted and waited upon
with no apparent terminus or resolution
unless what's poured into it includes you

7.

as in "a substantial portion of a larger manifest"—

someone's singing and singing and someone's
not there all day it's an awkward moment
outside in the coming night a tired tree
rubbing itself against a younger one

every few minutes it creaks like an opening door

Reality Misplaced by Truth

1.

I look inside my compass	I see
a world that goes on	without me
because I love too much	I can't love
all those darty fish	in his pants
they see I enjoy them	it will stop
the barnyard's full of messages	the chickens wrote
and they always said	the same things
it wasn't	the only language I lived in
mice had things to say	but mostly
so quickly at night	the chickens erased it
it's not something told	in the darkness
but something held	for the darkness
I'm still	something I don't recognize

2.

when I
I wasn't thinking about the way you

after the dream about you falling into
my house seemed full of

you weren't able to explain what it
so I

then there was a lull in the
screaming all the way back to

it couldn't have been any
but the emptiness just fell out like

and somehow the thing itself took over my
displacing everything I had tried to

3.
his thumb is talking   again
no one listens   to such pressure

inside the finger's lateral coffin   like water aimed and
a child's boat   floating on it

I look inside my compass and   I see without reason
a world goes on   without me

I make this thing   and I live in it
and I call it my home   only when no one listens

which is always brilliant   but it's warm enough
and never famous   for waiting

4.
I think I should sleep
but my body's doing my thinking for me.
I think I should eat
if I can't sleep, which I've done before to
relax my dreaming,

but that only gurgled me awake.
I think I should stop
thinking, of course, but I don't know
how to resolve
this quandary without sleeping between
thoughts and dreams,
which never open the same way twice.
I see myself in the mirror
and think, *This could be a dream* until
I think that I'm thinking.

5.
For reasons taller than wide, I decide
to sleep in the tree though the stability
of my decision remains a matter of opinion,
and my whim stretched out on its limb
creeps further and further from sleep.

I imagine falling and crawling away
for help and a painful stay of the execution
of my folly in its oddly diminution,
embarrassed by the caress of stray
fate and by rampant hubris kissed.

The tree does not climb its leaf
only to sleep but celebrates the brief
of the sun falling daily to awakenings,
fueled by more reliable fancy, bringing
tree after tree more slowly to earth.

At the edge of the dream, I finally fall
to that sleep and not to gravity at all,

and I do not remember gleaning
what I found there or how unfair
I was to its gracious departure.

6.

In the story I tell myself out walking when I cannot sleep, Grandmother Stick carries the baby to the center of the room, where everyone watches her trying to put a wig back together. A cat attempts to enter and is chased off by wooden spoons. Now it's grand- mother's turn to examine her feathers. "If I wear my hat to bed, perhaps I shall not fall down the stairs," thinks Papa, but no one will speak of it.

The long finger enlarges the hole. Dinner is red and does not keep Grandfather from sweating. "Newspapers are better than porridge," says Papa with his smiling bread- winner's face. Grandfather can't even keep a piece of food on his fork. He saves the comics for dessert and uses his fingers, despite the annoyed clicking of Papa's knuckles. The finger worries the hole still larger.

It's the next day, and they're gone now. Some of our parts are different, and our silence is louder. We're modern and pretend to be happy in a different way. We wear new travel stickers and leopard skin underwear. Our shoes don't match, and we still fall down the stairs, but we don't complain. The old man next door bangs on the TV set and shakes his head and shakes Mama's red leather boots. How did he get them? The TV says snow and more snow, and we don't know what that means. Outside, the Gothic cathedral points to the moon. Our names roll up the television, and we are done telling our story. (We left some of it behind with only the idea of a button.)

7.

Selected competitor nails a chickenhead to the wall. Rubber
fingers. Small red beetles crawling from his lunchbox. Beady
blue eyes. Puts the egg back inside the bird. Young boy egg, I
seem to be certain. His donation is a carriage pulled by snails.
Albino rats begin playing Go with blue stones.

(the swift tap of tiny canes curled down from the bodied umbrel-
las of leaves cantering across the macadam unbridled an impos-
sible whistle pitched nearly above the ear nearly out and away)

(something gregarious and skeletal in the limbs the trailing flags
of champion koi fins sparkling coins in the sunlight's accidental
invasions exploding delicately on the unwrinkled fabric of idyllic
ponds)

8.

I can't wrestle myself from harm
with the foolish safety I often pray away from
when the pin plays to its final firm embrace

(the last dregs of a fine white tea,
the dry hollow bodies on the sill
of bee and fly caught waking early)

as if something were saying *Certain*
experiences have settled for me,
and I cannot keep them safe.

9.

the words are light   like a mist drifting
across something   delicately to stay here

on that leaf   in the wooden bucket full
of slippers at the doorstep of soft misplaced directions

you didn't need to ask   where you weren't going
suddenly I'm another year old when we've only been nibbling

Scavenger

Inside the tree that resembles me,
evaporation has more patience.

Now I put down my stone,
falling slowly into it.

I can't give you any more than
this dark rag fluttering.

Was that you the rain found
naked in your clothing?

(all those little legs of rain walking
across the forgotten roof)

I catch the fly, and I say,
"Frog, lookie here," and I try
not to mention the broken wing.

What miracle was I escaping?

There are some things you can see
more clearly from a distance.

IV. Shaking Hands with Children

Red's Blues

a dog came up to me that night out of the blue
—Gerald Stern

reds in the lettuce tracts
reds in the beans
reds that face facts
and reds that dream

red for the lights that keep us
from the cold slab's unsignaled rush
red for the swollen swamp's disgust
and red for the bullfrog's booming trust

one red for evening
and one for blood
one more for believing
and one for the dove

and lots of little reds like ants gone wrong
that look black until you peer closer
and notice the little bodies strung
from the darkness folding here

red with an odor of rot
and reds all over the sunrise
reds like time's furniture collapsing hot
red all day like a dog glides

still intent on dogging and once again it's evening
as we call to the furred and wandering crew
and red slinks aboard his swampboat's yearning
neglected and howling darker its runaway blue

Seagulls Marching Before the Tide

big big sadness you live in
comes out and says
Not Now and Maybe Never
like you haven't met them

undone I exist beyond
bits of bud and eye of pollen
generously gendered and air-railed
(aural mist lifting its tentative engine
from grass throats and avian tinnitus)

bigger than the box I put big in
to hold it in my possibles

nobody knows me inside myself but
something horrible for a while now

what interests me is not me
it's the place where I am
when I'm not here

I tell the bird not to open itself
but it has me to absent welcome
feathered being-warmth
that means no return

such as involuntary rocks for example
or the war there is swept inward
and not released until the sand lifts

towards shore and separates salt water
greens and tears open an allowance or

succession of ancient pacing
we refer to as renewal

Self Portrait, in Absentia

we skinny girls never left

intention in our paintings
stumbling wind from which
somebody's drunken
Geographic's
Amazon became second wind
for third and we were

the late strewn
cold crept quickly to
father throwing down National
Rwanda for first base the
albino hummingbirds migrating
home to white Antarctica

home where nobody else wanted us

never alone together
everyone but myself I have
and I put the wrong books in it
ancestors those bloated
streets of Petershead and
hagus and acting out

but always lonely attracting
a busy library
my distinguished bloody
bagpipers celebrating
Aberdeen with grog and
off-color jokes

so inexperienced no one understood

charging slowly into each
intricately ornamented
sheep's bladder while
hiding a dirk in every fold of
big morbid unopened
death so often it's difficult

battle still blowing
melody out of a
yelling in Gaelic and
flagged wool with one
history of family
to catalog the fallen in

our thin dreary book so we created beautiful lies

in another section of

in between where content seems
sometimes to show
my connections to them
tenuous mutual interests and
proximity and I often find

books on happiness
squeezed dry
to ignore neighbors
the ones I should be ignoring
which contain not only
confused opinions but mere
invalid considerations

concerning the pleasures that exist between death and ancestors

instead I prefer
the stack of romance
I forgot to take to the

exciting the awful world outside

which I am missing by reading
I've discovered gravities

comment at length upon
magazines in the corner
shut-ins who need to know
how sleep
appears and fits among
possibility
such glorious garbage
but the miracles

that occur when the community disperses and the individuals

rise to meet the dust
beyond its apparent station

talking it over realizing
growing heavy and cold with

nuances of thin air and

skinny young girls like me

already gently voyaging
that's when they all start
again
what they've done and
this burden they wish to
share but
a muscled flank or a kind
word or
all three would fly if they
could and

sometimes they awaken according to legends and fairytales

we haven't ceased telling
propositions I intended to drop
eaten from me while considering
how to
not come to any conclusion
sympathetic the whole thing

you'd want to wear to bed

I'm still offering up the cool
I'm a plate you could have
clean up after yourself and

you could have been that
anticipated jewelry some-
thing
in case a star visited or
maybe

it's enough if something friendly wants to participate in our
undergarments

Seven Answers Without Questions

a suture of insects
dining at the wound

I want fresh teeth and fresh nails
I want a list of impossible symptoms

the grass still won't abandon
its earthy apparatus for moving
slowly from one place to another

we're here to betray me with forgiveness
who gets to be beautiful becomes unknown

farewell to the used-up hair farewell
to the relegation of parts farewell to
a mothful of separation spilling and

the broken speculation's worn fenders gumming
the mouthful of tender that brought us here

Several Islands Have Appeared and Swimming Is Possible

Let's say there wasn't any other way
let's say my sisters stood by the river and waved
hello and goodbye it was all the same
but sometimes it dropped its leaves and
we just waited sometimes it pointed
every direction at once without going

and the moment had only its way with me
a gang of them made up one
and it knew something I didn't
but it didn't understand each other I
admit I wanted to know them
and I didn't want it to leave me alone

my stories come back marked *not at this address* or *moved and owes me money* or *try another riverbank* or *no one even vaguely resembling this has ever lived here* and the wind's hot hand begins reaching beneath the earth's freshly woven clothing after a season of distance and cool brushing

domestic geese nervous about the sunshine after so much gray shake it off like the dust of an old attic while the turtles shuffle onto the bobbing driftwood climbing over each other to let light dry them their little bundled piles of white turd drying to paper and dreaming wondering what they can't remember

I had to wait for something outside   to come in
after something inside   had gone out
the distance was greater than   before
the breadcrumb trail   my thoughts had been
picked up and   swallowed by a crow
happy with himself   and the unexpected way the
                                        world provides

She Told Me She Needed Some Space

I dug up the occupied shoebox
because I had
previously arranged
a conclusion which fell down
not once did I imagine
the cat hadn't needed much space

to find my cat
in its questions about travel
and I simply arrived at
the hole and
I could have lived there only
in order to travel

it wasn't something
I invited the leaves to keep
unto themselves against the wind
promises spilled open
and for one endless moment
there that just was

I could have built
right on top of scratching
and I offered
mammalian buttons unfastened
because something was
not there

I tried not to be
too many daybreaks
there wasn't
anything but I
with my tendency
holding back

myself still raining but
whispering and
a holding to
grew heavier and leaning
to hold back
I chilled

there weren't any lights on
because the lights were
switches with
tendencies not to hold

in the house
all falling off
conclusions like
something back without a
reason

what I could have learned like
if only I had been traveling around

something nearly inside this
reasonably nearby

and my mother's boyfriend
sitting quietly inside

where once a cat
had been entered as if
part of a discussion with
a size 13 coffin shoe

I thought about stopping her
how I didn't want to interfere

with the fine collection
I had uncovered
toward something
mine even if I had lifted

something like the flashlight
of nocturnal occupational
intellectual flowerbeds of
strain to get far enough to
be about letting them express
they've done that

a gentle murder of roses

those rowdy smiles that weren't
leaving their almost behind
its unexpected performance as

how much I had forgotten
the decomposition of

already returning me to
the hole I had encouraged to
appear
that I thought belonged
in another realm of this
my mother putting her hands in
and then she began walking

but I think about this
among a lot of complicated
aspects
of feline mystery
within my cat's progress
which was not
its preoccupied singular
vision

that illuminates the discourse
hazards still sleeping before
dawn I can't
recognize their potential to
themselves again
since night took up sleep
and

insinuated Lorca and wasn't
about
needing to die again to be
staged once more in
a disappearance that
reminded me
clandestinely about
memory so I took

everything I had
and opened up
a name I had lived with in
a serial survivalist group
for joy and pain
everything

myself up to Godmart
an accounting under
Idaho where I had survived
which wanted me prepared
being nearly into
already happened

I had to admit to the members that
sort of journey smell with
time continually passing seemed
an access point as if
it but wanted just to travel in
a space I didn't know was

my cat's remainder was a
reward and seemed enough
to periodically light
from darkness I wasn't
what I was looking for
still looking for me

Since I Can't Paint Landscapes I Arrange the Furniture

I won't pretend to know what the stars say, but
it's not what I hear at night when I listen and wonder
where I fit in this overwhelming darkness and then
say something I learned in the light like an informant
waiting for those I live with every day to leave
me on the other side, where silence fits.

I can't even open a coat or replace an open door
with a closed one or mount the step after.
I can't stop a bill from going unpaid, but
I'll ask a couple of clouds to drop by and
rub themselves gently against the little
lake-like surface of the goldfish bowl.

Enter softening threats and rumpled goings on.
Enter innocuous burdens and temptations.

I get myself together and I generate motion
I arrive at myself and find my date disengaged,
but I participate freely. I advance the cause of
something I've come upon in my sleep that remains.

Back then the rain perished, and I waited
to become saturated with its absence
before setting sail inside my snug dry shell.

What she wants is in the pond, and it comes out
only when it wants to, and she comes out to meet it,

only when she wants to, and if she meets someone
on the way to the pond, then that too must be
the pond coming out, if she wants to, only she
would never call it love, but slip into it and wait
for it to return in the proper relation of tables.

Shaking Hands with Children

There's a dish of them okay

with no lid

still there's no excuse
tall and tall again
silly

fat enough as
their beanstalks breach
clouds of hope

already there's pale smoke
from the limbs of
fuzzy white pimples

blossoming
the cherry tree
popping each day open

there's exuberance careening

like a reckless polka

the children are singing:
it fits under the door
what do you think of that

The light loves the floor
but the dark is fat
and here's the adult

hand's opposing whale
between longer thinner
fish that can't live that way

breaching
less cuticled
there between and poking out

like the children's nose game
extending his flesh
prongs

there's a father
shovel's flexible sensitivity
there are parents

at the most promiscuous airports
magical gestured
no longer themselves

remembering
children half waking
and touching

V. To Bumble and Be

Contemplation of a Small Speckled Egg Frozen into a Whiskey Glass

Sometime in March the embarrassed green spears
    admit their intrusions, soften and open up,
their floppy green hats hung from the sides of tender heads,
    their penchant for windy sambas barely hidden.
Sleepy snow geese get lazier and seem to melt right into the
ground,
    where worms are forming their gentle armies
and scouting the dangerous sidewalks and wide sculptured lawns.
    Valuable pebbles thrown by bored children and held
all winter above the heads of fish fall to a soft warming bed of
swollen
    hand-shaped leaves and whatever the fish leave behind.
There's only one wet God, and he's trying to touch all the lost
    listeners who seem to be ignoring nearly everything
but the soggy snuggle of something forgotten in last fall's rush
    to dry up the mistaken tears and turn the dust white.

By July the lake's larval children have started leaving, and the trail
    can sometimes be seen in the passing mornings
that seem to worship them for a few minutes like a herd of
confused ghosts
    over the surface of the wide earthen bucket of life
that held them all spring in abeyance while they slipped in and out of
    the necessary gossip of gills and bladders.
If there are parents beyond the clouds, they must be quietly
inserting
    tiny little notes of rainy forgiveness in the children's
seasonal cloud-buckets while they send them off to learn what

matters.
     And so they come and go, each day others returning,
while the once spear-headed violators of soil continue to gobble the fallen
     and send them down, away from more obvious rewards,
under the melting armies of animal waste, dead leaves, weed mash,
     and into the passports healthy beasts call vegetation.

Soon enough, the new earthy masks pop up, cut and drying right there
     on the face of all that travels in the dark and demand
sugar or something to keep aside acid intent, quickly devouring
     the shell of innocence already flaking away
from the bright chubby visage of forever that makes us give and give,
     even as we smile and smile and send it away.
And now the earth stops pushing and lets *the slowly risen* sweeten
     and the travelers on its bounteous preserve
hold back the wealth and adjust the flow over the course of the taking away.
     In this there is another innocence, for we know not
how the giving of patience and the assimilation of the endless mystery
     might correspond to the early dark of such knowing.
Too soon we may think and discover we have consumed each other
     in the name of support to find being there alone is not being there.

And finally it descends upon us again, the leveling pride of hungry white
     researchers of cold domains reexamining the stilled herd.
We look and look again and see what we've missed in the flurry of
     winded musings, but we still may not understand it,
and the trail goes cold until we stop and consider where we've been,
     and where we're going appears there and moves
into the unsuspecting bodies and opens out like a rotting fruit

grown sweeter for all its loss and hidden increase,
and we eat of the silence and pure cold that prospers without us,
and we are no longer ourselves, nor our bodies,
journeying out there on the ice and hard dry crust of experience
to meet us where we have lived without knowing
since before any interruptions from the bodies we walk on, or in,
and we do not need to call it "soul" or even "reward."

Small Towns Naked in Their Welcome

I believe the sky-covered Bruges
        and the rain was failing it took
                three of my parts to hold me up

Oh O dear blue you can have me now skied and sung down
        the bruised king of Belgium perched on the potato cart
                hiding the prince's collection of attractive yellow tulips

                lost in bearable performance

milk garments inside the crippled peddler
        offering a little impossible reward more like
                the royal neighbor's limping cat eating bees

there was a tongue there I seemed to
        have left my tongue in I was just about to
                start something we were too close to see it

the grandfather strata humming in his
        kiss-flaked under-being transpiring
                with the jerky exactitude of ants

                performing in bearable loss

Oh cousin oh of a building
        I lived in then constrained
                by sunshine and cloud cover

this is where my nowhere arrives

a way of coming into the body going out
    a celestial navigation without arrows or coins

bearable with others offering

Some Good Advice

Sometimes think goofy. Bring several
       pigs with wheels to the teddy bear's
             big tea every other lasting Tuesday.

Don't Despair. Visit the Department of
       Partial Certainty. Request another
             certificate of renewed clarification.

Put a hitch in the tear gear.
       Entertain all the giggling pants.
             Hold back. You could be abiding.

(He says *Yrs,* and he says *Bugger*
       the law, and he *says Offered im*
             a good slap in the old meat, I did.)

In the sandbox the ocean arrives—
       children with eyepatches strutting,
             forcing each other to walk the plank.

Sprinkle a finely diced rose on a sultry pear.
       Go looking for its partner. Offer trepidations
             like roasted chestnuts to the nearest laundromat.

(the tree articulating in the almost absent wind)

The dogwood blossoms bark at the breeze,
       which keeps right on stealing their voices.
             That was the color the sky meant by falling.

(the patient tree articulating in the absent wind)

That one's a nipper then, eh?
(frightened and wet)
To the guilty, all are guilty.

Someone Else Entirely/The Woman Without Her Name

she hadn't been frozen   in sleepy shimmers of
ancient silk

but when she walked   something was always left
behind

her eyebrows seemed   to learn more than we were
saying

something like time passing   but it didn't have any new
ideas

where it was going   considering the alternatives
she had already been   one thought in front of the
other

[the gymnasts were not allowed to carry *Jello*
no woodcarvers had arrived late
no bookstores were opening]

it's like a fire of laughter   spreading through the
treetops

in everyone and falling down   and sputtering out and
finally

glowing long after the danger   curled safe after its animal
has eaten another meal   but I say that it still offers
almost nothing   nothing to say

[I am not often available to my own
queries when
spoken correctly they appear to be water resting
upon one another after not resting upon one another

and it seems
where there might be more
it doesn't seem to care
and not that much of it lingers
like this or like anything it likes
it seems to be asking how
not one causing the other but
you have to decide

that's the way it is inside
we could do with it but
if we do it's what it is
not that you were ever
less than the problem
do I deal with you
once reduced and no more
what it's worth

       if you could be someone else
   you could see yourself asking
even as you answer the question]

I was finally ready
to say what it was
my lips or just words and

to begin I tried
but I couldn't put together
my secret thoughts I had
many

useless things to say and only
in the territory of the events

I released them all
I was assembling

    [objects of such transparency could not be found in
harmony
   and seemed to be climbing the simplicity of feeling allowed
like something mysterious on her stepfather's breath]

what remained was to wonder
would it feel like another family
would it need me to stay open

does the word *love* have no English equivalent
if I step on a worm do I need to exclaim *I don't understand you*
are we protected by the unbelievability of our mistakes

[how do I know if you're mine frog
I've had children all over the swamp
rain falling on sidewalks and driveways]

rain falling on rain
slumped in his intentions and falling further
the kind of place that had no opinions

natural dirt-colored hair
taken by the slightest alternative
giddy with almost hope

Sometimes It's My Mind That Wanders

That summer the bumble of a bee bobbling a mirror
seemed as if it held my suspect memory, but

sometimes I seem to be just a good bit of garment
slipped down on appearances to where I live inside
with my lips showing fashionably and late for living
into and flung gaily to the welcome face of another,
cheekier restraint. *Untoward,* an older appendage
might say, but I'm practiced at deceiving myself,

and from time to time, I get tired of my retreating
mind and take it to visit vegetables in the garden
as if they couldn't know what I've forgotten, and
I hear the cool whisper of a carrot beneath the stairs,
and I direct a watermelon's sloppy barge onto the
cutting board for my favorite corrections as if

I could have the hands of a surgeon, and I visit the
restless potatoes in their lair. You can hear them
winter nights galloping across the cellar, dark eyes
all over their bodies reaching colorlessly for the earth
that holds them this season when their limbs collect
memories of pale children kept beneath winter.

Of course they resent my body's arrogance, the slowest
cringe of all beside the turnips, but have you seen the
brutal smile of a squash squat down on the hill and
climb slowly inside, holding to itself the way water
holds to water, even while molding to its container?
So little is needed, they remind me, but it's needed

always, and I realize I can do better, and I take myself
outside. I should have had something on my mind that
isn't my mind, the way I have something on my head
now that isn't my head, but the word *hat* pops up like
a badly chosen clue that's supposed to lead somewhere
else and doesn't. That's the way a mind works when it

tires of containment. I can find no reason to disbelieve in it
the leaves coming back from the trees to tell me of the silence
they were so carefully electing, so I tell them about one of
the holidays I'd removed my feet from when I was too much
surrendered. By this time it's nearly dawn and the dew begins
kissing, so we drink, the leaves and I, till there's a bit less

pity, and black flaps of birds begin discussing
the smell of winter like flags out over the meadow,
then punctuate the useless phone lines. I haven't called
for anyone except myself, and he hasn't showed up,
except as a vegetable and a vegetable and another
vegetable wandering past where the mind rests, and he

puts the leash back on and lets me walk him back, which
isn't at all where I thought it was with my legs, so I admit that
he's not as tired of me as I was of him, and I enter myself before
he can open the door my little thinking door is in and surround
occupied *me* with *inside myself*, where I have nevertheless
learned to operate with my body dragging me around

while the mirror I started with reflects a different persistence
that needs only a singular reliable impulse to bumble and be.

Song of Meat

I'm in love with you because I appreciate nature.
If you knew me better you'd be frightened.
If everything you do leaves a frantic trail then
don't do anything. Better not be someone.

If you're well-liked, they most certainly will find you.
What they will do is not specific but entirely and blithely
sad. Partly brilliant was that man or thought I was and,
he didn't take care of himself. I wasn't really living in

his breaking body. He had much to say, but when he opened
the discrepancies, his mouth left the points unable to chew.
His smell came back with every gesture. Cabbage
spoke softly of how long it had been left in the juices.

He celebrated the contradictions. We lived by them,
the oblivion of his own salvations, offered by the satiated
participants who wanted to save more than themselves,
stirred to his dirt and dream bedroom by heroic folly and

a drifting mind. Naked everything looked like
it belonged to someone else. Perhaps good fortune did
as well, when he washed the rain to give thanks and
actually carried himself away, his voice wild and high

and far too confident. I considered carefully how
he would win me, neurotic tortured absolutes
springy as kid goats. He was right about
the future, but it wasn't his future. Nor mine.

I'm telling you this because he's gone now
and you're here. You wouldn't have seen yourself
in him as I did. You don't pretend to know.
Neither would you have tried to save him,

who didn't want any saving, just as you don't
for yourself want any encouragement. Still,
you know he needed it, you know you don't.
Why don't you let Nature correct you?

Steps

down here where people work all day
      we have things to do that
         do things to us

      at night the streetlights blossom and
    sidewalks are plum-colored and fall away
and we become their accidents of ripeness

    the people in the sky think
they know where they're going

but we have tickets and friends
    with keys whispering and doors
        that wait in their own lives

        there's someone inside these
    possibilities with another purpose
  looking for something in a wallet
purchased in 1973 that taught him

there's so much to do here that isn't
    a questionable treasure chest stolen
        from a king trying to buy time

      you can always watch those
  who are best at this because
they forget what they're doing

there's something to
        drag out of you that takes
                nobody to do it especially not you

                one is too much and none is more
        several others are finding themselves
with you inside them and they're all

inside themselves where you are
pilfering

sometimes I wish the clouds
        would talk to me and when
                they do I realize it's not
                        something I wanted to hear

                you fit them best
when you wait too long

Still Life with Goldfish

You might wonder if I didn't solve
my problems. I might wonder if I did.

There were still some things that pleased me.
Half and half again, the sky's white heart shrunk.

It's what a mountain of you did, the lifted body
wrapped in water like a comfortable fish

all the way to the mouth of another civilization.
Your thoughts may have wandered from the bowl.

There are places to hide where everyone can see you.
There's a freedom that loves gravity. Sunlight made me

greedy and tired. You could go there and find something
happening slowly enough to let you live.

The Unapologetic Excess Made Me Wince

Once there was a hole in the ground,
and I fell into its emptiness.

I filled the hole with myself.
The emptiness remained.

It had nothing to do with tears
or drinking or the end of the world
or a hole in the ground.

I only said that to make you fall in,
which makes the emptiness fall out,

which makes a hole no longer a hole,
which makes nature happy although
it doesn't care that we did it,

which makes me happy, which
leaves the ground alone with its hole.

9 789388 319881